W9-BRD-301

BASIL

A
S P R I G
O F
Basil

Twenty-five
Classic Recipes
by
JOHN MIDGLEY

Illustrated *by*
IAN SIDAWAY

A Bulfinch Press Book
Little, Brown and Company

BOSTON • NEW YORK • TORONTO • LONDON

ACKNOWLEDGEMENTS
The author thanks Sue Midgley and Helen Parker for checking the text,
and Ian Sidaway for his excellent illustrations.

FURTHER READING
The Complete Book of Herbs, by Lesley Bremness (Dorling Kindersley)
The Encyclopedia of Herbs, Spices and Flavourings, by Elisabeth Lambert Ortiz
(Dorling Kindersley)
The Herb Book, by Arabella Boxer and Philippa Black (Octopus)
The Herb Garden, by Sarah Garland (Windward)
History of the English Herb Garden, by Kay Sanecki (Ward Lock)
How to Grow and Use Herbs, by Ann Bonar and Daphne MacCarthy
(Ward Lock)
Wisley Handbooks: Culinary Herbs, by Mary Page and William Stearn
(Cassell for the RHS)

Text copyright © 1994 by John Midgley
Illustrations copyright © 1994 by Ian Sidaway

All rights reserved. No part of this book may be reproduced
in any form or by any electronic or mechanical means,
including information storage and retrieval systems,
without permission in writing from the publisher,
except by a reviewer who may quote brief passages in a review.

First Edition
ISBN 0-8212-2097-7
A CIP catalogue record for this book is available
from the British Library

Conceived and designed by Andrew Barron and John Midgley

Published simultaneously in the United States of America
by Bulfinch Press, an imprint and trademark of
Little, Brown and Company (Inc.),
in Great Britain by Little, Brown and Company (UK) Ltd.
and in Canada by Little, Brown & Company (Canada) Limited

PRINTED AND BOUND IN ITALY

$\mathcal{C}$ONTENTS

BASIL

Basil belongs to the *Labiatae* group of plants, a large family that includes sage, marjoram, rosemary, thyme, balm, mint, savory, bergamot, hyssop and lavender. Native to India and south-east Asia, basil has been cultivated there for many thousands of years, and has been grown in Europe for over two thousand years. It has religious, mystical and ceremonial significance for many cultures. For Hindus it has long been a sacred herb, and the ancient Greeks called it *basilikon* which means 'regal'. In Greece, bush basil is still kept by the threshold to ward off the evil eye, and, more practically, to repel flies!

The principal varieties are sweet basil (*Ocimum basilicum*); dark opal basil (*Ocimum basilicum purpurascens*); bush basil (*Ocimum minimum*); holy basil (*Ocimum sanctum*); lemon basil (*Ocimum basilicum citriodorum*); lettuce-leaf basil (*Ocimum basilicum crispum*); cinnamon basil (*Ocimum basilicum 'Cinnamon'*) and camphor basil (*Ocimum kilimandsharium*).

Sweet basil is the most familiar and versatile variety, and is used extensively in Italian and Provençal cooking. It has quite large, glossy leaves and small white flowers (or pink, in the case of the opal hybrid, making it a good ornamental plant). In a Mediterranean climate, sweet basil can reach a height of 1 m (3¼ ft). Bush basil is equally fragrant but much more compact, with very small leaves and tiny white flowers. It can grow up to 30 cm (1 ft). Holy basil is widely used in south-east Asia, and is very fragrant with small, hairy leaves that are less fragile than those of the

other basil varieties. As their names suggest, lemon and camphor basil are also powerfully aromatic, and lettuce-leaf basil, while useful to the cook, is also a good ornamental herb.

The fragrance of basil is attributable to its essential oil which is widely used in perfumery and aromatherapy; it is said to be a calmant, effective against stress and insomnia.

GROWING BASIL

Although the plants are self-seeding in the tropics, else-
where basil is treated as a tender or half-hardy annual. Even
in warm Mediterranean countries, the seeds are sown relatively late, in April or May, and the plants are protected
until May or June. All basil varieties are suitable for planting in herb gardens, as well as in pots, troughs and window
boxes. In fact, they are perfect container herbs and do well
in pots and tubs on well-sheltered, sunny patios. Hot,
sunny window sills provide the ideal environment since
basil thrives behind glass in hot-house conditions.

The seeds germinate quite quickly – often within a
fortnight – if kept warm. They can also be sown directly
into rich, well-drained soil in a sheltered position in full sun
or partial shade but only when all danger of frost has passed
and the soil temperature is hospitably warm; conditions
which in temperate countries such as Britain are unlikely to
occur before late May or early June. Basil can be very useful
to gardeners in companion planting; the flowers are
extremely attractive to bees, so they aid pollination of other
plants.

As root disturbance stunts growth, seeds can be sown
directly into containers, and the seedlings subsequently
thinned out. I sow the seeds into organic, phostrogen-
enriched root pots and then transplant them whole into the
soil or into larger pots without disturbing the roots. Alternatively, sow the seeds in a greenhouse or cold frame in
April and move the young plants out in June. Thin out
some seedlings to prevent overcrowding and keep the

plants warm and reasonably moist (but do not over-water as they are prone to 'damping-off' disease).

Potted basil plants are readily available nowadays. They can be transferred to a bed or planted up into larger pots. Whether sown from seed or ready-potted, basil plants need warmth and shelter to thrive; too many cool, rainy days will weaken them, as will cold winds. When such miserable conditions seem set in, it is a good idea to move the plants indoors until the sun reappears and temperatures improve. Hot weather stimulates the plants' aromatic oils, while in poor summers they tend to smell of cats! Plants should be watered regularly in hot spells, preferably in the cool of the early morning, and, if grown in containers, they must be well-drained as they dislike having waterlogged roots.

Once established, the growing tips should be pinched out to encourage bushy growth and to delay flowering. Regular picking for the kitchen will ensure this but if any growths do escape your attention and develop flowers they too should be pinched out. Fortunately, the aromatic oils are most concentrated in the growing tops. If you are as fond of basil as I am, you will need at least a dozen plants to maintain a supply throughout the summer. The plants will naturally die back in late September and any remaining green leaves can be then be stripped and frozen.,

COOKING WITH BASIL

A 'kingly' herb, according to its etymology, for me, basil is also the king of all herbs. Only rosemary and sage can evoke as successfully as basil the heat of a summer afternoon in Greece or Italy, where the air throbs soporifically with the chant of a million cicadas. The intense aroma and flavour of basil (described variously as warm, spicy, sweet, pungent, and clove-like) are a powerful reminder of a healthier, more relaxed Mediterranean lifestyle which revolves around the pleasures of the table.

Basil's closest culinary allies are tomatoes, olive oil, garlic, fresh summer vegetables, beans, eggs, cheeses, fish, and poultry. The herb is frequently added to salads, soups, and curries (particularly south-east Asian ones made with coconut milk). Yet most cooks would agree that basil's apotheosis is found in *Pesto Genovese* it is hard to imagine a more satisfying balance of flavours, aromas and textures than those achieved in this sublime marriage of pounded basil, garlic, pine nuts, cheese, olive oil, and pasta.

Tearing basil leaves releases their bewitching aroma, and whether used in leaf form or as pesto, always introduce basil just before serving. In my opinion, the use of dried basil is sacrilegious. Fortunately, the fresh leaves freeze very well and can be stored in plastic food bags. Although their colour darkens on thawing, much of their fragrance remains. Basil leaves may also be preserved in olive oil for a short time and will impart a wonderful flavour and scent to the oil. As the cold is damaging and hastens deterioration, basil should not be stored in the refrigerator. Ideally, therefore, basil leaves should be picked (or bought) and used on the same day.

Many of the following recipes are traditional dishes culled from different countries, from Thailand to Italy and France, with some of my own creations added to the pot for good measure.

9

ASIL OIL

Basil leaves can be preserved for a fortnight or so in a little olive oil, while also flavouring the oil. Wash a generous handful of fresh basil leaves and shake off the water droplets. Pat them dry with kitchen paper (paper towel). Bruise the basil lightly and put it into a clean glass bottle with a stopper. Fill with 225 ml/8 fl oz/1 cup extra virgin olive oil, ensuring that the leaves are covered. Leave to infuse for up to 2 weeks; the leaves can be used normally and the oil kept to flavour salads, soups and marinades.

BASIL VINEGAR

Heat 350 ml/12 fl oz/1¹⁄₂ cups white wine or cider vinegar in a pan. Before it boils, remove from the heat. Wash a small bunch of fresh basil leaves and shake them dry. Tear the leaves and stuff them into a clean glass bottle with a stopper. Fill with the vinegar and allow to cool. Screw on the lid and leave to infuse for 2 weeks. Strain the vinegar into a fresh bottle, adding a fresh sprig of basil. Use the vinegar to flavour salads and marinades.

BASIL BUTTER

I like to dress baked potatoes with pats of basil butter. It is also very good on boiled vegetables. Additionally, use basil butter to baste roast poultry, stir it into soups and sauces, or toss freshly boiled, drained pasta with a generous quantity of basil butter, adding freshly milled black pepper and parmesan cheese.

110 g/4 oz unsalted butter, at room temperature
¹⁄₂ clove of garlic, peeled and very finely chopped
handful of fresh basil, washed and shredded
pinch of salt and freshly milled black pepper

Mash the butter very thoroughly. Mix in the remaining ingredients and mash again. Shape into a neat roll, wrap loosely in foil and refrigerate. Cut off individual sections as required.

$\mathcal{B}$RUSCHETTA AL BASILICO

Similar to *pa'amb tomaquet* from the Catalonian region of Spain, *bruschetta* is a very popular Italian snack. It is made with slices of country bread that are lightly toasted over a hearth fire, rubbed with crushed garlic and juicy tomatoes, then liberally dressed with extra virgin olive oil. Freshly torn basil leaves complement *bruschetta* wonderfully. This recipe serves 4–6 people as an appetizer.

1 crusty loaf (about 350 g / 12 oz)
2 cloves of garlic, peeled and crushed
4–6 very ripe, juicy tomatoes, halved
extra virgin olive oil or basil oil
salt
12 basil leaves

Cut the loaf at a slight diagonal into 2 cm/1 inch slices (about 12 in total). Toast each slice lightly on both sides. Rub one side of each slice with garlic, then squash the tomatoes onto the rubbed sides. Drizzle liberally with the oil and sprinkle with salt. Tear the basil leaves and scatter them over the *bruschetta*. Serve at once, while still very warm.

$\mathscr{S}$ T U F F E D   S U N - D R I E D
T O M A T O E S

Serve these delicious bite-sized canapés with a small selection of *antipasti*, including some thinly sliced Parma ham or salami. Use a jar of sun-dried tomatoes in oil (*pomodori secchi sott'olio*) or buy them loose and soften them yourself as follows:

225 g/8 oz sun-dried tomatoes
450 ml/16 fl oz/2 cups water
2 tbs wine vinegar
2 cloves of garlic, peeled and crushed
handful of fresh basil leaves
olive oil

Put the tomatoes into a glass or ceramic bowl and pour the water and vinegar over them. Soak for at least 2 hours to soften them. Drain thoroughly, put them in a preserving jar and insert the garlic and basil. Fill the jar with olive oil and keep for at least 1 week.

350 g/12 oz sun-dried tomatoes in oil
225 g/8 oz mozzarella di bufala or Italian cow's milk mozzarella
16 fresh basil leaves, torn
1 tbs pine nuts
extra virgin olive oil

Arrange the tomatoes on a serving dish, the concave sides facing upwards. Cut the mozzarella into small strips that will fit into the tomato halves. Put a piece of mozzarella, some basil leaf fragments and a few pine nuts into each tomato half. Drizzle sparingly with olive oil and serve.

13

ASIL AND CHIVE
VINAIGRETTE

Although this herbal vinaigrette is a particularly delicious dressing for leafy green salads it is equally suitable for other salads. The recipe makes enough vinaigrette to dress a salad large enough for 6 people.

small bunch of fresh basil
small bunch of fresh chives
6 tbs extra virgin olive oil
2 tbs sherry vinegar or balsamic vinegar
salt and freshly milled black pepper

Wash the herbs and shake off as much moisture as possible. Pat them dry with kitchen paper (paper towel). Chop them as finely as possible with a sharp knife or a *mezzaluna*. Beat the oil and vinegar in a small bowl. Mix in a pinch of salt and some freshly milled black pepper to taste, and stir in the herbs. Set aside for a few minutes but once the salad has been tossed it should be served immediately or the vinaigrette will cause the leaves to 'wilt'.

14

$\mathscr{C}$OURGETTES (ZUCCHINI) AND BASIL SALAD

This delicious *antipasto* is a speciality of the Jewish community of Rome. Accompanied by crusty bread, it makes an excellent appetizer. Alternatively, serve the salad with a selection of small dishes, avoiding oily or marinated ones. Makes enough for 2 persons.

> *900 g/2 lb courgettes, washed*
> *salt*
> *sunflower* or *peanut oil*
> *1 clove of garlic, peeled and finely chopped*
> *large handful of fresh basil leaves, torn*
> *salt and freshly milled black pepper*
> *3 tbs extra virgin olive oil*
> *sherry vinegar* or *balsamic vinegar.*

Slice the courgettes into discs, about 1 cm/$\frac{1}{2}$ inch thick. Sprinkle them with salt and leave them to 'bleed' for 30 minutes. Rinse the courgettes and pat them dry with kitchen paper (paper towel).

Heat a generous layer of oil to smoking point in a large, well-seasoned frying pan. Without crowding the pan, fry the courgettes in batches, allowing both sides to turn golden-brown. Transfer the courgettes with a slotted spoon to a plate lined with kitchen paper.

Line a china, glass or terracotta bowl with a layer of courgettes. Sprinkle with a little chopped garlic and some torn basil leaves, season, and drizzle with olive oil and a few drops of vinegar. Repeat until the ingredients have been used up and serve at room temperature.

$\mathscr{I}$NSALATA TRICOLORE

This salad, which honours the Italian flag, is especially delicious when it has been prepared with genuine buffalo milk mozzarella. Make it in high summer, when tomatoes are ripe, sweet and fragrant; otherwise, you may substitute cherry tomatoes which are more readily available at other times of the year and are usually well-flavoured. Be generous with the basil, and tear it just before you serve to release its bewitching aroma. Accompanied by good crusty bread to mop up the juices, this serves 4 as an appetizer or 2 as a light meal.

675 g / 1½ lb ripe tomatoes, sliced
275 g / 10 oz mozzarella di bufala, drained and sliced
generous handful of fresh basil leaves, torn up
salt and freshly milled black pepper
4 tbs extra virgin olive oil

Arrange the tomatoes in attractive, overlapping rings on a wide serving platter. Top each one with mozzarella slices and scatter the torn up basil over them. Season and drizzle with olive oil.

ANZANELLA

Bread salads are found in many parts of Italy and have evolved from simple peasants' and farm labourers' snacks. Hard bread would be taken to the fields or groves and softened with water, wine or vinegar and olive oil, and eaten with an onion or garlic and with whatever vegetables were available. *Panzanella* is a Tuscan bread salad from the Chianti hills that can be made with any well-flavoured country bread. Serves 4 as an appetizer.

1 stale crusty loaf (about 350 g/12 oz)
350 g/12 oz ripe, juicy tomatoes, washed
1 red salad onion, peeled
1 clove of garlic, peeled and finely chopped
heart of a Cos (romaine) lettuce, washed, shaken dry
and shredded
small Mediterranean cucumber, peeled and diced small
generous handful of fresh basil leaves, torn
110 ml/4 fl oz/½ cup extra virgin olive oil
3 tbs red wine vinegar
salt and freshly milled black pepper

Tear the bread into smallish chunks and soak them in a little water. Squeeze out the moisture and put the bread into a serving bowl. Dice the tomatoes and add them to the bowl. Halve the onion from top to bottom, slice the hemispheres thinly and add to the bowl. Add the garlic, lettuce, cucumber and torn basil leaves and mix everything thoroughly. Beat the oil with the vinegar and seasoning and pour over the salad. Mix again, cover and chill for 30 minutes–1 hour to allow the flavours to develop.

BEAN SOUP

Use fresh haricot (navy) beans whenever they are in season. Otherwise, substitute canned beans. (You can also soak 575 g/1¼ lb dried haricot beans overnight, boil them for 1 hour, drain and proceed with the recipe.) Since this Greek soup is very similar to minestrone, you could stir in a few tablespoons of *pesto* just before serving instead of the basil leaves. Makes enough soup for 6 people.

1kg/2¼ lb fresh haricot beans, unshelled
or 900 g/2 lb canned beans, rinsed and drained
110 ml/4 fl oz/½ cup olive oil
handful of fresh parsley, chopped
350 g/12 oz fresh, very ripe tomatoes, peeled and chopped
or 200 g/7 oz canned plum tomatoes, chopped
1 medium onion, peeled and chopped
2 sticks (ribs) of celery, with leaves still attached, chopped
350 g/12 oz new potatoes, diced
salt and freshly milled black pepper
1¾ litres/3 pints water
small handful of fresh basil leaves, torn

Shell the beans, if fresh. Boil them for 20 minutes, drain and set them aside. Heat the olive oil in a large pot. Add the parsley and the remaining vegetables (including canned beans or dried beans that have been soaked and boiled). Season well and cover with water. Bring to the boil, cover the pot and simmer for 45 minutes. Mix in the basil, check the seasoning and serve straight away with crusty bread.

$\mathscr{R}$IGATONI WITH FRESH PLUM TOMATOES

Fresh plum tomatoes are only really ripe in high summer; peel them with a sharp or serrated knife, and dice the flesh. Otherwise, substitute a 400 g/14 oz can of plum tomatoes (chopped) or 225 ml/8 fl oz/1 cup bottled crushed tomatoes.

10 very ripe, fresh plum tomatoes, peeled and diced
3 cloves of garlic, peeled and chopped
4 tbs extra virgin olive oil
salt and freshly milled black pepper
400 g/14 oz rigatoni or other large, hollow pasta shapes
2 handfuls of fresh basil leaves
75 g/3 oz freshly grated parmesan cheese

Combine the tomatoes, garlic, olive oil, salt and pepper in a pan and bring them to a simmer.

While the sauce is cooking, bring plenty of salted water to a fast boil in a large pot and drop in the pasta, stirring well. Cook until *al dente*.

Drain the pasta and combine it with the sauce, scattering the basil over it. Mix thoroughly and serve with the freshly grated parmesan cheese.

$\mathscr{P}$ESTO GENOVESE

In the Liguria region of Italy, *pesto* is the favoured pasta sauce; it is also stirred into soups and added to flavour vegetables and *gnocchi*. Waxy salad potatoes and, occasionally, green beans are added to *pesto* when it is served with pasta. It may come as a surprise that, although very satisfying, the result is far from heavy. Ribbon noodles called *trenette* are preferred by purists but *fettuccine* or *tagliatelle* are a good substitute. (If you know a good delicatessen that makes it on the premises, or if you make it yourself at home, do use fresh pasta but remember that it cooks more quickly.) Serving 4, this makes a complete meal.

PASTA
350 g/12 oz new potatoes, cleaned but unpeeled
225 g/8 oz good quality dried egg fettuccine
or 450 g/1 lb good quality fresh fettuccine
175 g/6 oz green beans, topped and tailed

Bring a very large pot of salted water to a fast boil. Immerse the potatoes, and after they have boiled for about 10 minutes, add the dried pasta (wait until the potatoes are nearly tender before adding fresh pasta.) Mix well, and boil until the pasta is *al dente*. While they are cooking, separately boil the green beans until just tender.

PESTO
small bunch of fresh basil
2 cloves of garlic, peeled and sliced
pinch of salt and freshly milled black pepper
75 g/3 oz pine nuts
225 ml/8 fl oz/1 cup extra virgin olive oil
75 g/3 oz freshly grated pecorino sardo or parmesan cheese

While the other ingredients are boiling, pound or process the basil with the garlic, salt, pepper and pine nuts. Add a little olive oil as soon as you have a pulp. Keep pounding or processing while adding the remaining oil in a thin stream. (If using a mortar and pestle, pound the *pesto* quite thoroughly with just a few drops of the oil before stirring in the rest.)

Drain the pasta, potatoes and beans when they are ready. Stir half of the cheese into the *pesto*. Slice the potatoes and arrange them around the rim of a large, warmed serving dish. Return the pasta to the empty cooking pot. Mix in the *pesto* and the green beans, ensuring that all the pasta strands are well coated with the *pesto*. Transfer the pasta to the serving dish, sprinkle with the remaining cheese, and serve immediately.

GNOCCHI AL PESTO

Make the *pesto* sauce as in the preceding recipe and combine thoroughly with these home-made potato *gnocchi* which serve 4 people.

675 g/1½ lb floury potatoes, peeled
4 tbs milk
2 tbs olive oil
½ tsp salt
350 g/12 oz/3 cups plain (all-purpose) flour
75 g/3 oz freshly grated parmesan cheese

Put the potatoes and plenty of water into a large pan and bring to a boil. Cover and boil the potatoes until they are cooked. Pour away the water, add the milk, olive oil and salt and quickly mash the potatoes until they are completely smooth.

Allow the mashed potatoes to cool a little, then combine them with most of the flour, kneading thoroughly with floured hands. (The dough should be smooth and elastic.) Flour a work surface, break up the dough into balls and roll these out into long snakes, each one about the width of a finger. Cut into 1½ cm/⅔ inch squares and dust lightly with flour. Bring plenty of salted water to the boil. Press each square of dough against the prongs of a fork and let it drop straight into the boiling water. (Do this quickly, in batches, to ensure even cooking.) The *gnocchi* cook very quickly and should be scooped out with a slotted spoon as soon as they float to the surface. Transfer all the cooked *gnocchi* to a warmed serving bowl, combine thoroughly with the *pesto* and serve with parmesan cheese.

 USILLI ALLA CRUDAIOLA

This recipe could not be simpler or, apart from the marinating time, quicker to prepare. You need very ripe, sweet tomatoes so this is really a dish for high summer. Alternatively, add 2 tbs of tomato *passata* and a pinch of sugar to less than perfect tomatoes and proceed with the recipe. Substitute other ribbed pasta such as *penne rigate* if *fusilli* are unavailable; *spaghetti*, *spaghettini*, *bucatini* and *linguine* are also good vehicles for this delicious raw sauce.

675 g / 1½ lb ripe fresh tomatoes
2 cloves of garlic, peeled and finely chopped
20 black olives, pitted and chopped
6 tbs extra virgin olive oil
salt and freshly milled black pepper
400 g / 14 oz fusilli
generous handful of fresh basil leaves, torn
75 g / 3 oz piece of parmesan, freshly grated

Peel the tomatoes with a very sharp, serrated knife (or plunge them in boiling water for 30 seconds to loosen their skins). Dice the flesh. In a wide serving bowl combine the tomatoes with the garlic, olives and olive oil. Season and mix again. Set aside for an hour or so to allow the flavours to develop.

Bring a very large pot of salted water to a rolling boil. Immerse the pasta and mix. Cook until *al dente*. Drain and combine the pasta with the tomato mixture and freshly torn basil leaves. Serve immediately with the parmesan and some crusty bread.

$\mathcal{P}$ASTICCIO OF BASIL AND GOAT'S CHEESE

A *pasticcio* is a layered cake of partly-cooked pasta that is mixed with flavouring ingredients and baked or grilled (broiled). This recipe calls for fat, hollow pasta shapes such as *rigatoni*. The goat's cheese gives an agreeable tang to the strained fresh or canned tomato sauce which is delightfully complemented by an abundance of aromatic basil. This serves 4 as an appetizer, or 2 as a light lunch or supper.

4 tbs extra virgin olive oil
1 medium onion, peeled and chopped
1 stick (rib) of celery, thinly sliced
1 carrot, scrubbed and thinly sliced
1 clove of garlic, peeled and finely chopped
675 g/1½ lb fresh plum tomatoes, peeled and chopped
or 400 g/14 oz chopped canned plum tomatoes
salt and freshly milled black pepper
4 tbs white wine
350 g/12 oz rigatoni
generous handful of fresh basil leaves, washed and torn
100 g/3½ oz soft goat's cheese, crusts removed, and diced
2 tbs extra virgin olive oil

Heat the oil in a pan. Soften the onion, celery and carrot for about 4 minutes. Add the garlic and tomatoes, season, and cook for 10 minutes (if fresh tomatoes are used), or 15 minutes (for canned tomatoes). When they have reduced to a thick sauce, sieve it through a wire strainer, moistening the pulp with the wine to assist the extraction. Put the strained sauce to one side.

Cook the pasta in a very large pot of rapidly boiling salted water until *al dente*. Meanwhile, pre-heat the grill (broiler) and oil a wide, shallow oven dish. Drain the pasta, and transfer it to the oven dish. Quickly re-heat the tomato sauce, adding half of the basil, and combine thoroughly with the pasta. Sprinkle over the goat's cheese and the remaining basil. Drizzle with the remaining olive oil and grill until the cheese has melted and the surface of the pasta is golden-brown. Serve immediately with crusty bread.

GRILLED (BROILED) POLENTA WITH TOMATO AND BASIL

This recipe calls for blocks of cooked, set *polenta*. The blocks are fried, then combined with tomato sauce, grated cheese and fresh basil leaves, and finally toasted briefly under the grill (broiler). Accompanied by a leafy salad, this makes an excellent light lunch or supper for 2 or an appetizer for 4 people.

Follow the cooking instructions on the *polenta* packet; you will need about $1\frac{1}{2}$ litres/$2\frac{2}{3}$ pints of water for a packet of Italian 'instant' (pre-cooked) *polenta*. Pour the *polenta* in a thin, steady stream into a pot of rapidly boiling salted water, stirring all the while. When the *polenta* is cooked (after about 5 minutes), it will be very thick and will come away from the sides of the pot. Add a few knobs of butter, several tablespoons of freshly grated parmesan and season with plenty of freshly milled black pepper. Mix thoroughly and spread out the *polenta* onto a clean wooden chopping

board to a thickness of about 5 cm/2 inches. When it has cooled and solidified, slice it into even blocks, each about 5 cm/2 inches square. (Any left over blocks can be put into plastic food bags and refrigerated or frozen.)

olive oil, for frying
8 blocks of cooked, set polenta *(see above)*
400 g/14 oz can of plum tomatoes, chopped
4 tbs extra virgin olive oil
2 cloves of garlic, peeled and chopped
salt and freshly milled black pepper
6 tbs freshly grated parmesan cheese
12 large fresh basil leaves, torn

Heat a thin layer of olive oil to smoking point in a non-stick frying pan. Carefully add the blocks of *polenta* in batches. Fry them over a medium heat, until a light golden crust forms. Turn them over and fry the other side. Remove and drain on kitchen paper (paper towel).

Cook the tomatoes over a medium heat for 10-15 minutes, mixing them well with the extra virgin olive oil, garlic, salt and pepper. Pre-heat the grill (broiler).

Lightly oil 2 (or 4) ramekins and cover the base with a thin layer of tomato sauce. Divide the fried *polenta* equally between the ramekins, spoon over a little more tomato sauce, and cover with a good sprinkling of grated cheese. Decorate generously with freshly-torn basil leaves. Grill until the cheese is flecked golden-brown.

$\mathscr{L}$ÉGUMES FARÇIS
AU BASILIC

In Provençe summer vegetables such as sweet peppers, courgettes (zucchini) and tomatoes are prepared in numerous ways. Here, they are stuffed with a meatless mixture that includes plenty of fresh basil, then baked until tender, providing an ample meal for 4 people.

4 ripe marmande or beefsteak tomatoes
4 sweet red peppers
4 large courgettes
6 tbs olive oil
1 medium onion, peeled and chopped
3 cloves of garlic, peeled and finely chopped
salt and freshly milled black pepper
350 g/12 oz/2½ cups cooked rice
75 g/3 oz pine nuts, toasted
75 g/3 oz raisins
8 sun-dried tomato halves, chopped
glass of white wine
small bunch of fresh basil, chopped
handful of fresh parsley, washed and chopped
2 tbs tomato purée (paste)
560 ml/1 pint/2 cups vegetable stock (broth)

Pre-heat the oven to 190° C/375° F/gas mark 5.

Wash the vegetables. Slice the tops off the tomatoes and discard them. Carefully cut out the central flesh, taking care not to break the walls. Chop the flesh and set it aside. Remove and discard the caps, pith and the prominent parts of the pithy inner ribs of the peppers. Top and tail the courgettes (or baby marrows) and halve them from end to

28

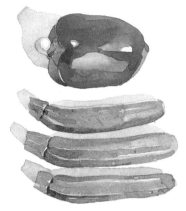

end. With a teaspoon carefully scoop out and discard the seedy centres; you should have unbroken 'shells'.

Heat the oil in a frying pan and gently fry the peppers for 10 minutes, turning them over a few times. Remove the peppers and wipe off the oil. Re-heat the pan and sauté the onion and garlic until soft and pale golden. Add the chopped tomato, season and cook for 5 minutes. Set the tomato mixture aside. In a bowl, combine the rice with the pine nuts, raisins, sun-dried tomatoes, wine, half of the basil and all the parsley. Season well and mix again. Spread a little cooked tomato over the base of 2 oven dishes. Arrange the vegetables on top, the cavities facing upwards. Stuff them with the rice mixture and cover with the remaining tomato mixture. Dissolve the tomato purée in the stock and pour over the vegetables. Bake for 45 minutes, or until tender. Sprinkle with the remaining basil and serve hot.

$\mathcal{P}$IZZA MARGHERITA

This, the simplest of pizzas, is authentically Neapolitan. With its relatively simple topping of tomato, mozzarella, fruity olive oil and fresh basil, it is quite delicious. The dough makes 4 smallish pizzas with a crisp, thin crust.

DOUGH
½ packet of dried yeast (about 1½ tsp)
225 ml/8 fl oz/1 cup of hot water
350 g/12 oz/3 cups plain (all-purpose) flour
1 tsp salt
1 tbs olive oil

Dissolve the yeast in the water. (This is unnecessary if you are using fast-action yeast but check the instructions on the

packet.) Mix the flour, salt and olive oil in a bowl. Gradually add the yeast mixture, kneading all the while either by hand, or with a mixer fitted with dough hooks. When the dough is smooth and elastic (after about 15 minutes if kneading by hand, or after 5 minutes' machine-kneading), transfer it to an oiled container (first dust your hands and the dough with flour), cover with a clean cloth and leave in a warm place for an hour or until the dough has risen appreciably. Dust your hands, a work surface and a rolling pin with flour. Divide the dough into 2 equal balls and divide each ball in half. Roll out the 4 pieces of dough into discs about 20 cm/8 inches in diameter, turning them as you roll so that the shapes are circular.

Pre-heat the oven to 220° C/425° F/gas mark 7.

TOPPING
140 ml/5 fl oz/²⁄₃ cup tomato passata
225 g/8 oz Italian mozzarella, diced
salt and freshly milled black pepper
fruity olive oil
16 basil leaves, torn

Place the pizza bases on 2 flat, oiled baking sheets or on individual oiled tart pans. Spread out a quarter of the tomato over each pizza base. Dot evenly with mozzarella, season and drizzle a little olive oil over them. Bake for 15–20 minutes. Swap the trays to ensure even cooking and check that the edges and base are firm and lightly browned. Decorate with the basil fragments and serve immediately.

$\mathscr{P}$ISSALADIÈRE

This traditional onion, anchovy and black olive tart from
Nice is closely related to the pizzas of Provence's eastern
neighbour, although the similarity in names is coincidental
(*pissala* is the local name for anchovy paste). I use a stan-
dard pizza dough for the base. Serves 6, accompanied by a
salad.

ONION TOPPING
1½ kg/3½ lb onions, peeled
110 ml/4 fl oz/½ cup olive oil
4 cloves of garlic, peeled and thickly sliced
salt and freshly milled black pepper
generous handful of fresh basil, washed and torn
2 tsp thyme, chopped
about 20 anchovy fillets
handful of pitted black olives
olive oil

Halve the onions from top to bottom. Slice each hemisphere
very thinly. Heat the olive oil in a large pan. Add the onions
and garlic and cook very gently for 45 minutes–1 hour, stirring from time to time. They should become sweet and
brown. Remove them with a slotted spoon and put them
into a bowl. Season, mix in the herbs, reserving a few basil
leaves for decoration, and set aside.

DOUGH BASE
(see *Pizza margherita* recipe on page 30)

Pre-heat the oven to 220° C/425° F/gas mark 7.
    Make the dough exactly as directed but do not divide

32

the ball once kneaded. Roll out the dough ball to a thickness of 6 mm/$\frac{1}{4}$ inch (thicker than for a pizza). Place the dough sheet on an oiled baking pan. (Traditionally, the base is circular but you can also use a rectangular tart pan.) Pinch up the edges with thumb and forefinger to create a raised rim. Bake for about 20 minutes, or until the crust is golden-brown.

Pile the onion on to the dough base, spreading it out evenly to reach the rim. Arrange a diamond-shaped lattice-work of anchovy fillets on top and place an olive in the centre of each diamond. Drizzle with olive oil and bake for 15 minutes. Decorate with the reserved basil leaves, cut the *pissaladière* into wedges, and serve very hot.

PANE FRATTAU

This is a delicious, wholesome example of *la cucina povera*, the daily fare of ordinary people in rural districts of Italy. *Pane frattau* is traditionally made with Sardinian *carta da musica* bread, so-called because it is brittle, paper-thin and stacked like leaves of sheet music. Thin Middle Eastern or Indian unleavened breads make a good substitute if they are first heated in the oven to harden them slightly. Large sheets of crispbread are also suitable. These quantities serve 2 people.

8 layers of carta da musica
or 2 pittas or 4 large crispbreads
6 tbs extra virgin olive oil
1 clove of garlic, peeled and finely chopped
110 ml/4 fl oz/¹/₂ cup tomato passata
or finely chopped canned plum tomatoes
salt and freshly milled black pepper
8 basil leaves
2 very fresh free-range eggs
50 g/2 oz freshly grated parmesan or pecorino sardo *cheese*

Warm the bread in a cool oven (140° C/275° F/gas mark 1) while you prepare the remaining ingredients. In a small pan heat 2 tbs olive oil, the garlic, tomato and seasoning. Simmer for about 5 minutes to thicken the sauce. Add the basil leaves and put to one side.

Heat the remaining oil to smoking point in a non-stick frying pan. Carefully slip in the eggs and fry them until the whites are set, basting with spoonfuls of hot oil. Remove

the eggs and divide them with a knife (or fry each one separately). Divide the bread into 2 portions, spread a layer of tomato over each, sprinkle with cheese and top with a fried egg. Serve immediately.

35

$\mathcal{P}$ARMIGIANA DI ZUCCHINI

Prepared with fresh, sun-ripened plum tomatoes, glossy, firm courgettes (zucchini) and headily scented with basil, this is simple summer cooking at its best. You may substitute aubergines (eggplants) which are the preferred ingredient in the dish's native Campania region of Italy.

800 g/1¾ lb courgettes or 2 large aubergines, washed
salt
3 tbs extra virgin olive oil
675 g/1½ lb ripe plum tomatoes, peeled and chopped
or 400 g/14 oz canned tomatoes, chopped
2 cloves of garlic, peeled and chopped
salt and freshly milled black pepper
flour, to coat the aubergines
olive oil, for frying
large handful of fresh basil leaves, washed and torn
225 g/8 oz Italian mozzarella, diced
75 g/3 oz piece of parmesan, grated

Top and tail the courgettes (or aubergines) and slice them evenly from end to end; the long slices should be about ½ cm/¼ inch thick. Sprinkle them with salt and let them 'bleed' for 30 minutes. (If you are using small, very firm vegetables, this should be unnecessary.)

Meanwhile, heat the extra virgin olive oil, tomatoes, and garlic in a pan. Season, cover and simmer for about 10 minutes, then cook uncovered for 5 more minutes. Pre-heat the oven to 200° C/400° F/gas mark 6.

Rinse the slices and pat them dry. Dip them in flour. Heat a generous layer of olive oil in a large non-stick frying pan. Fry them in batches until golden-brown. Drain and transfer them to a plate lined with kitchen paper (paper towel).

Spread a layer of tomato sauce over the base of a wide, shallow oven dish measuring about 23 cm/9 inches in diameter. Scatter a few torn basil leaves over the layer of sauce. Cover with a layer of fried courgettes (or aubergines). Dot with mozzarella, and sprinkle with parmesan. Repeat until all the ingredients have been used up, and finish with some mozzarella and parmesan, a little tomato sauce and some basil leaves.

Bake until the cheese has melted and coloured golden-brown (15–20 minutes). Carefully drain off any surplus fat, allow to rest for 5–10 minutes and serve warm or tepid with plenty of crusty bread.

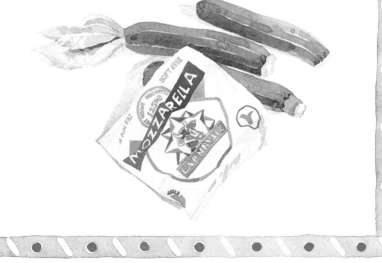

$\mathscr{R}$ED MULLET BAKED WITH BASIL

Firm, white-fleshed fish such as red mullet are delicious cooked with basil, especially when their enticing, complementary aromas are preserved in parcels. Served with boiled new potatoes and a salad or some green beans, this makes enough for 4 people.

olive oil
4 medium red mullet, filleted
salt and freshly milled black pepper
handful of fresh basil
2 cloves of garlic, peeled and finely chopped
4 shallots, peeled and very finely chopped
675 g/1½ lb ripe tomatoes, peeled and chopped
extra virgin olive oil
2 lemons, quartered

Pre-heat the oven to 200° C/400° F/gas mark 6. Prepare 4 individual rectangles of foil or greaseproof paper, each one large enough to envelope a fish fillet. Wipe each rectangle with olive oil. Season the fish.

Scatter half of the basil and half of the garlic, shallots and tomatoes over the oiled sheets. Season, then lay a fish fillet on top. Arrange the remaining basil and vegetables over the fish, season again and drizzle 3 tsp of extra virgin olive oil over each portion. Seal the parcels, folding the edges tightly.

Bake until the flesh has begun to flake but remains moist and succulent (about 15 minutes). Serve immediately, still tightly wrapped, and garnish with lemon quarters.

CHICKEN CURRY WITH PEPPERCORNS AND BASIL

This sublime Thai curry is delicious with plain boiled rice and mangetouts (snow peas) stir-fried with garlic and a little soy or oyster sauce. Thai 'red' curry paste is very fragrant when it has been freshly made. However, ready-made paste is available in oriental supermarkets or you can substitute Indian brands of curry paste. This serves 4 people.

1 chicken or 4 chicken breasts
2 tbs freshly milled black peppercorns
4 tbs plain (all-purpose) flour
4 tbs peanut oil
2 tbs curry paste (preferably Thai 'red')
400 ml/14 fl oz can of (unsweetened) coconut milk
1 tbs lime juice or lemon juice
1 tbs Thai fish sauce
1 tbs soy sauce
1 tbs sugar
75 g/3 oz peanuts, crushed
handful of holy basil or sweet basil, torn

Skin the chicken and cut the flesh off the bone; cut into even cubes each about 3 cm/1¼ inches square. Roll the chicken first in the pepper, then in flour. Heat the oil in a wok to smoking point. Add the chicken pieces and stir-fry until lightly coloured. Add the curry paste and stir-fry for 1 minute, then pour in the liquids, the sugar and the peanuts. Stir the mixture for about 4 minutes while it thickens. Mix in the basil and serve immediately.

ℳ ARINATED STIR-FRIED
CHICKEN WITH FRIED BASIL

An exotic but simple dish for 4 people that is sour, tangy and redolent of basil. After a period of marination, the quickly-cooked chicken is topped with crisp, fried basil. Serve with plain boiled rice and a stir-fried vegetable.

MARINADE
1 chicken, or 4 chicken breasts
1 tbs rice vinegar
1 tbs Thai fish sauce
2 tsp light soy sauce
$\frac{1}{2}$ tsp cayenne
1 tbs peanut oil
4 fresh basil leaves, torn

Skin the chicken, cut the flesh off the bone and slice it into thin strips. Mix all the marinade ingredients together thoroughly. Set aside for 20–30 minutes. Meanwhile, prepare the remaining ingredients.

2 tbs peanut oil
12 fresh basil leaves
4 cloves of garlic, peeled and thinly sliced
white part of 4 spring onions (scallions), thickly sliced
juice of a lime
1 tsp sugar
1 tbs Thai fish sauce
2 fresh chili peppers, washed and sliced
50 g/2 oz cashews

Heat the oil in a wok to smoking point. Throw in the basil leaves. They will crackle and immediately turn crisp.

Remove them with a slotted spoon before they burn and set them aside. Remove the chicken from the marinade.

Re-heat the wok to smoking point and add the garlic. Stir once and add the spring onions and the chicken. Toss the chicken pieces around in the wok until they turn opaque, then add the remaining ingredients, stirring well. Continue to stir-fry for 3 minutes, by which time the chicken should be cooked. Transfer to a heated serving bowl and top with the fried basil. Serve immediately.

BASIL